YOUR KNOWLEDGE HAS

- We will publish your bachelor's and
  master's thesis, essays and papers

- Your own eBook and book -
  sold worldwide in all relevant shops

- Earn money with each sale

Upload your text at www.GRIN.com
and publish for free

Bibliographic information published by the German National Library:

The German National Library lists this publication in the National Bibliography; detailed bibliographic data are available on the Internet at http://dnb.dnb.de .

This book is copyright material and must not be copied, reproduced, transferred, distributed, leased, licensed or publicly performed or used in any way except as specifically permitted in writing by the publishers, as allowed under the terms and conditions under which it was purchased or as strictly permitted by applicable copyright law. Any unauthorized distribution or use of this text may be a direct infringement of the author s and publisher s rights and those responsible may be liable in law accordingly.

Imprint:

Copyright © 2019 GRIN Verlag
Print and binding: Books on Demand GmbH, Norderstedt Germany
ISBN: 9783668983908

This book at GRIN:

https://www.grin.com/document/491406

Gabriel Kabanda

Analysis and design of algorithms. A critical comparison of different works on algorithms

GRIN Verlag

GRIN - Your knowledge has value

Since its foundation in 1998, GRIN has specialized in publishing academic texts by students, college teachers and other academics as e-book and printed book. The website www.grin.com is an ideal platform for presenting term papers, final papers, scientific essays, dissertations and specialist books.

Visit us on the internet:

http://www.grin.com/

http://www.facebook.com/grincom

http://www.twitter.com/grin_com

REVIEW OF ALGORITHMS DESIGN AND ANALYSIS

Gabriel Kabanda

ABSTRACT

The paper presents an analytical exposition, critical context and integrative conclusion on the six major text books on Algorithms Design and Analysis. An algorithm is a sequence of unambiguous instructions for solving a problem, and is used for obtaining a required output for any legitimate input in a finite amount of time. Algorithms can be considered as procedural solutions to problems where the focus is on correctness and efficiency. The important problem types are sorting, searching, string processing, graph problems, combinatorial problems, geometric problems, and numerical problems. Divide-and-conquer is a general algorithm design technique that solves a problem by dividing it into several smaller sub-problems of the same type and about the same size, solving each of them recursively, and then combining their solutions to get a solution to the original problem. The brute-force approach to combinatorial problems is the exhaustive search, which generates each and every combinatorial object of the problem following a selection of those of them that satisfy all the constraints until a desired object is found. Although the main tool for analyzing the time efficiency of a nonrecursive algorithm is to set up a sum expressing the number of executions of its basic operation and ascertain the sum's order of growth, the main tool for analyzing the time efficiency of a recursive algorithm is to set up a recurrence relation expressing the number of executions of its basic operation and ascertain the solution's order of growth. A graph with directions on its edges is called a digraph. To list vertices of a digraph in an order such that for every edge of the digraph, the vertex it starts at is listed before the vertex it points to, is the topological sorting problem which has a solution if and only if a digraph is a dag (directed acyclic graph), i.e., it has no directed cycles. The topological sorting problem can be solved by two algorithms, one based on depth-first search; and the second based on a direct application of the decrease-by-one technique. The three major variations of decrease-and-conquer are: decrease-by-a-constant, most often by one (e.g., insertion sort) decrease-by-a-constant-factor, most often by the factor of two (e.g., binary search) variable-size-decrease (e.g., Euclid's algorithm).

1. ANALYTICAL EXPOSITION

The paper presents an analytical exposition, critical context and integrative conclusion on the six major text books on Algorithms Design and Analysis. Algorithms form the heart of Computer Science in general. An algorithm is simply a set of steps to accomplish or complete a task that is described precisely enough that a computer can run it. Levitin, A. (2011, p.3) defines an algorithm as a sequence of unambiguous instructions for solving a problem, and is used for obtaining a required output for any legitimate input in a finite amount of time. Generally, algorithms are procedural solutions to problems. On a similar note, an algorithm is any well-defined computational procedure that takes some values as input and produces some values as output (Mount, D.M., 2003, p.2). According to Levitin, A. (2011, p.11), an algorithm design technique solves problems algorithmically as a general approach to solving problems from different areas of computing. Erickson, J. (2019) puts it more precisely that an algorithm is an explicit, precise, unambiguous, mechanically-executable sequence of elementary instructions, usually intended to accomplish a specific purpose. An algorithm is an efficient method that can be expressed within finite amount of time and space, and is independent from any programming languages. Algorithms are independent of any programming language, machine, system, or compiler. An instance of the problem is specified by an input which the algorithm solves. Algorithms can be specified in a natural language or pseudocode, and they can also be implemented as computer programs where the focus is on correctness and efficiency (Mount, D.M., 2003, p.2). The most important problem types where algorithms are used are sorting, searching, string processing, graph problems, combinatorial problems, geometric problems, and numerical problems. Among several ways to classify algorithms, there are two principal alternatives according to Levitin, A. (2005, p.38) and these are to group algorithms according to:

❖ the types of problems they solve

❖ underlying design techniques they are based upon.

Kleinberg, J., and Tardos,, E. (2005, p.1) in their book on Algorithm Design introduced in Chapter One an algorithmic problem that precisely illustrates many of the themes in Algorithm Design, called the Stable Matching Problem. According to Kleinberg, J., and Tardos, E. (2005, p.4), matchings and perfect matchings arise naturally in modeling a wide range of algorithmic problems and these recur frequently throughout the book. The Stable Matching Problem originated from the self-enforcing need to design a college admissions process, or a job recruiting process. For a given set of preferences among employers and applicants, the key question is how can we assign applicants to employers so that for every employer E, and every applicant A who is not scheduled to work for E, at least one of the following two things is the case?

(i) E prefers every one of its accepted applicants to A; or

(ii) A prefers her current situation over working for employer E.

Kleinberg, J., and Tardos, E. (2005, p.4) presented the Gale-Shapley problem where a perfect matching corresponds simply to a way of pairing off the men with the women, in such a way that everyone ends up married to somebody, and nobody is married to more than one person in such a way that there is neither polygamy nor singlehood. Generally, we perform the following types of analysis on algorithms taken on any instance of size a:

❖ Worst-case (the maximum number of steps)

❖ Best-case (the minimum number of steps)

❖ Average case (an average number of steps)

❖ Amortized (a sequence of operations applied to the input of size a averaged over time).

A particular scheme of organizing related data items is called a data structure (Levitin, A., 2011, p.25). Since algorithms operate on data, the issue of data structuring is critical for efficient algorithmic problem solving. The most important elementary data structures are the array and the linked list, which in turn are used for representing more abstract data structures such as the list, the stack, the queue, the graph (via its adjacency matrix or adjacency lists), the binary tree, and the set. An abstract data type (ADT) is an abstract collection of objects with several operations that can be performed on them (Levitin, A., 2011, p.39). Implementation of ADTs is achieved in modern object-oriented languages by means of classes.

The major focus in algorithms design is to find efficient algorithms for computational problems. An algorithm is efficient if it runs quickly when implemented on real input instances; achieves qualitatively better worst-case performance, at an analytical level, than brute-force search (Kleinberg, J., and Tardos,, E., 2005, p.33); or has a polynomial running time (Kleinberg, J., and Tardos,, E., 2005, p.35). *Time complexity* is a measure of time efficiency which indicates how fast an algorithm in question runs. *Space complexity* measures the space efficiency, which is the amount of memory units required by the algorithm in addition to the space needed for its input and output (Levitin, A., 2011, p.42). Whereas the time complexity is calculated from the count of the number of times the algorithm's basic operation is executed, space complexity is calculated from the count of extra memory units consumed by the algorithm. The worst-case efficiency of an algorithm is its efficiency which the algorithm runs the longest among all possible inputs of that size n (Levitin, A., 2011, p.47). The best-case efficiency of an algorithm is its efficiency which the algorithm runs the fastest among all possible inputs of that size (Levitin, A., 2011, p.48). Both time and space efficiencies are a function of the algorithm's input size. However, the efficiencies of some algorithms may differ significantly for inputs of the same size, and so we need to draw a distinction among the worst-case, average-case, and best-case efficiencies. An algorithm's running time may grow as its input size goes to infinity.The asymptotic orders of growth of functions expressing algorithm efficiencies are denoted by the notations O,Ω , and Θ which are are used to indicate and compare them. Without loss of generality, the efficiencies of a large number of algorithms are categorized into the following few classes: constant, logarithmic, linear, linearithmic, quadratic, cubic, and exponential (Levitin, A., 2011, p.95). Although the main tool for analyzing the time efficiency of a nonrecursive algorithm is to set up a sum expressing the number of executions of its basic operation and ascertain the sum's order of growth, the main tool for analyzing the time efficiency of a recursive algorithm is to set up a recurrence relation expressing the number of executions of its basic operation and ascertain the solution's order of growth.

A function t (n) is said to be in O(g(n)), denoted t (n) $\square$ O(g(n)), if t (n) is bounded above by some constant multiple of g(n) for all large n, i.e., if there exist some positive constant c and some non-negative integer n_0 such that

$$t (n) \leq cg(n) \text{ for all } n \geq n_0 \quad \text{(Levitin, A., 2011, p.53).}$$

A function t (n) is said to be in Ω(g(n)), denoted t (n) $\square \Omega$ (g(n)), if t (n) is bounded below by some positive constant multiple of g(n) for all large n,i.e., if there exist some positive constant c and some non-negative integer n_0 such that

$$t (n) \geq cg(n) \text{ for all } n \geq n_0 \quad \text{(Levitin, A., 2011, p.54).}$$

A function t (n) is said to be in Θ(g(n)), denoted t (n) $\square \Theta$ (g(n)), if t (n) is bounded both above and below by some positive constant multiples of g(n) for all large n, i.e., if there exist some positive constants c_1 and c_2 and some non-negative integer n_0 such that $c_2 g(n) \leq t (n) \leq c_1 g(n)$ for all $n \geq n_0$ (Levitin, A., 2011, p.54).

Levitin, A. (2011, p.95) observed that inefficiency of a recursive algorithm may be masked by succinctness. When every element is equal to the sum of its two immediate predecessor, this generates a sequence of integers called the Fibonacci numbers. Fibonacci numbers can be computed using several algorithms with drastically different efficiencies. Algorithm visualization occurs when images are used to convey useful information about the algorithms (Levitin, A., 2011, p.95). Algorithm visualization occurs in the form of either the static algorithm visualization or dynamic algorithm visualization (also called algorithm animation).

4

Brute force is a straightforward approach to solving a problem where it is usually directly based on the problem statement and definitions of the concepts involved (Levitin, A., 2011, p.97). The brute-force approach is known for its major on wide applicability and simplicity, but has a weakness concerning the subpar efficiency. A sorting algorithm is stable if two elements that are equal remain in the same relative position after sorting is completed (Mount, D.M., 2003, p.8). The following noted algorithms can be considered as examples of the brute force approach:

❖ definition-based algorithm for matrix multiplication

❖ selection sort

❖ sequential search

❖ straightforward string-matching algorithm

The brute-force approach to combinatorial problems is the exhaustive search, which generates each and every combinatorial object of the problem following a selection of those of them that satisfy all the constraints until a desired object is found. The exhaustive-search algorithms can be used to solve the traveling salesman problem, the knapsack problem, and the assignment problem, among others (Levitin, A., 2011, p.130). The exhaustive search has been found to be impractical for a majority of cases except a few instances of problems it can be applied to. The better alternatives are the two principal graph-traversal algorithms, Depth-first search (DFS) and breadth-first search (BFS). The investigation of many important properties of the graph can best be conducted by representing a graph in a form of a depth-first or breadth-first search forest. Both algorithms have the same time efficiency: $\Theta(|V|^2)$ for the adjacency matrix representation and $\Theta(|V|+|E|)$ for the adjacency list representation.

A general algorithm design technique called *Decrease-and-conquer*, exploits the relationship between a solution to a given instance of a problem and a solution to a smaller instance of the same problem. Further exploitation of the relationship can be done either top down (usually recursively) or bottom up (Levitin, A., 2011, p.167). The three major variations of decrease-and-conquer are:

❖ decrease-by-a-constant, most often by one (e.g., insertion sort)

❖ decrease-by-a-constant-factor, most often by the factor of two (e.g., binary search)

❖ variable-size-decrease (e.g., Euclid's algorithm)

A direct application of the decrease-(by one)-and-conquer technique to the sorting problem is *Insertion sort* (Levitin, A., 2011, p.167). Insertion sort is a $\Theta(n^2)$ algorithm both in the worst and average cases, but it is about twice as fast on average than in the worst case. The algorithm achieves a good performance on almost-sorted arrays.

A graph with directions on its edges is called a *digraph* (Levitin, A., 2011, p.168). To list vertices of a digraph in an order such that for every edge of the digraph, the vertex it starts at is listed before the vertex it points to, is the topological sorting problem which has a solution if and only if a digraph is a dag (directed acyclic graph), i.e., it has no directed cycles (Levitin, A., 2011, p.168). The the topological sorting problem can be solved by two algorithms, one based on depth-first search; and the second based on a direct application of the decrease-by-one technique. A natural approach to developing algorithms for generating elementary combinatorial objects is to use the decrease-by-one technique, where the minimal-change algorithms is the most efficient class of such algorithms. However, even the best algorithms are of practical interest only for very small instances of such problems as the number of combinatorial objects grows phenomenally.

When searching in a sorted array, the *Binary search* is a very efficient algorithm which is based on a decrease-by-a-constant-factor algorithm (Levitin, A., 2011, p.168). There are other examples which include exponentiation by squaring, identifying a fake coin with a balance scale, Russian peasant multiplication, and the Josephus problem. The size reduction varies from one iteration of the algorithm to another for some decrease-and-conquer algorithms. Common examples of such variable-size decrease algorithms include Euclid's algorithm, the partition-based algorithm for the selection problem, interpolation search, and searching and insertion in a binary search tree.

A general algorithm design technique that solves a problem by dividing it into several smaller sub-problems of the same type (about the same size), solving each of them recursively, and then combining their solutions to get a solution to the original problem is called the *Divide-and-conquer* (Levitin, A., 2011, p.198). There are a number of efficient algorithms that are based on this technique, in spite of its both inapplicability and inferiority to simpler algorithmic solutions. The Running time T (n) of many divide-and-conquer algorithms satisfies the recurrence T (n) = aT (n/b) + f (n). The Master Theorem establishes the order of growth of its solutions. According to Erickson, J. (2019, p.29), both *Mergesort* and *Quicksort* follow a general three-step pattern called divide and conquer, which entails the following steps:

1. Divide the given instance of the problem into several independent smaller instances of exactly the same problem.

2. Delegate each smaller instance to the Recursion Fairy.

3. Combine the solutions for the smaller instances into the final solution for the given instance.

Mergesort is a divide-and-conquer sorting algorithm, which works by dividing an input array into two halves, sorting them recursively, and then merging the two sorted halves to get the original array sorted (Levitin, A., 2011, p.198). The algorithm's time efficiency is in $\Theta(n \log n)$ in all cases, with the number of key comparisons being very close to the theoretical minimum. Its principal drawback is a significant extra storage requirement. MergeSort is a classical divide-and-conquer algorithm which works recursively. The array is split into two sub-arrays of roughly about the same size, these are sorted recursively and then the two sorted sub-arrays are merged together in $\Theta(n)$ time (Mount, D.M., 2003, p.9). MergeSort is a stable sorting algorithm. However, the MergeSort is the only algorithm that requires additional array storage (ignoring the recursion stack), and thus it is not in-place because the merging process merges the two arrays into a third array. Mount, D.M. (2003, p.9) argues that although it is possible to merge arrays in-place, it cannot be done in $\Theta(n)$ time. MergeSort correctly sorts any input array A[1 .. n] (Erickson, J., 2019, p.25). Erickson, J. (2019, p.25) presented the key steps to Mergesort as follows:

❖ Divide the input array into two sub-arrays of roughly equal size.

❖ Recursively mergesort each of the sub-arrays.

❖ Merge the newly-sorted sub-arrays into a single sorted array.

HeapSort is based on the implementation of a priority queue data structure, called a heap, which is an efficient structure. The operations of inserting a key are supported by a priority queue, and the element with the smallest key value is deleted in the process. A heap can be built for n keys in $\Theta(n)$ time, and the minimum key can be extracted in $\Theta(\log n)$ time (Mount, D.M., 2003, p.9). HeapSort is not stable but is an in-place sorting algorithm. A heap can allow you to extract the k smallest values in $\Theta(n + k \log n)$ time (Mount, D.M., 2003, p.9). A heap is advantageous in contexts where the priority of elements changes and each change of priority (key value) can be processed in $\Theta(\log n)$ time.

Quicksort, as a divide-and-conquer sorting algorithm, works by partitioning its input elements according to their value relative to some preselected element (Levitin, 2011, p.168). Quicksort is noted for its superior efficiency among *n log n* algorithms for sorting randomly ordered arrays but also for the quadratic worst-case efficiency. According to Mount, D.M. (2003, p.8), Quicksort works recursively, by first selecting a random "pivot value" from the array and then it partitions the array into elements that are less than and greater than the pivot. Quicksort then recursively sorts each part. QuickSort is widely regarded as the fastest of the fast sorting algorithms on modern machines. The inner loop of Quicksort compares elements against a single pivot value, which can be stored in a register for fast access. The other algorithms compare two elements in the array. Quicksort is an in-place sorting algorithm which uses no other array storage, but was observed by Mount, D.M. (2003, p.8) as not stable. Erickson, J. (2019, p.27) presents the key steps to Quicksort as follows:

❖ Choose a pivot element from the array.

❖ Partition the array into three sub-arrays containing the elements smaller than the pivot, the pivot element itself, and the elements larger than the pivot.

❖ Recursively quicksort the first and last sub-arrays.

Examples of the divide-and-conquer technique include the classic traversals of a binary tree (preorder, inorder, and postorder) and similar algorithms that require recursive processing of both left and right sub-trees (Levitin, A., 2011, p.168). All the empty sub-trees of a given tree can be replaced by special external nodes.

There is a divide-and-conquer algorithm for multiplying two n-digit integers that requires about $n^{1.585}$ one-digit multiplications. By exploiting the divide-and-conquer technique, Strassen's algorithm which normally requires seven multiplications to multiply two 2×2 matrices, this algorithm can multiply two $n \times n$ matrices with about $n^{2.807}$ multiplications. According to Levitin, A. (2011, p.198), the divide-and-conquer technique can be successfully applied to two important problems of computational geometry: the closest-pair problem and the convex-hull problem.

A *heap* is a binary tree where the keys are assigned to its nodes, with one key per node, subject to the following two conditions being met (Levitin, A., 2011, p.227):

1. The binary tree is simply complete (shape property)

2. The key in each node is greater than or equal to the keys in its children (the parental dominance or heap property).

Transform-and-conquer is the fourth general algorithm design (and problem-solving) strategy discussed by Levitin, A. (2011, p.250), which is a group of techniques based on the idea of transformation to a problem that is easier to solve. The three principal varieties of the transform-and-conquer strategy are:

❖ *Instance simplification*, which transforms an instance of a problem to an instance of the same problem with some special property that makes the problem easier to solve. Good examples of this strategy include list presorting, Gaussian elimination, and rotations in AVL trees.

❖ *Representation change,* this is where one representation of a problem's instance is changed to another representation of the same instance. Examples of this type include representation of a set by a 2-3 tree, heaps and heapsort, Horner's rule for polynomial evaluation, and two binary exponentiation algorithms.

❖ *Problem reduction*, this is where a given problem is transformed to another problem that can be solved by a known algorithm. Examples of this strategy include reductions to linear programming and reductions to graph problems.

A heap is an essentially complete binary tree with keys (one per node) satisfying the parental dominance requirement (Levitin, A., 2011, p.250). Heaps are binary trees which are normally implemented as arrays, and are most important for the efficient implementation of priority queues; they also underlie heapsort. Heapsort is a theoretically important sorting algorithm based on arranging elements of an array in a heap and then successively removing the largest element from a remaining heap. The algorithm's running time is in $O(n \log n)$ both in the worst case and in the average case; and it is in-place (Levitin, A., 2011, p.250). AVL trees are binary search trees that are always balanced to the extent possible for a binary tree where the balance is maintained by transformations of four types called rotations. All basic operations on AVL trees are in $O(\log n)$; which eliminates the bad worst-case efficiency of classic binary search trees. Levitin, A. (2011, p.250) argues that the 2-3 trees achieve a perfect balance in a search tree by allowing a node to contain up to two ordered keys and have up to three children. This idea can be generalized to yield very important *B-trees*.

Gaussian elimination is an algorithm for solving systems of linear equations, which solves a system by transforming it to an equivalent system with an upper-triangular coefficient matrix, which is easy to solve by back substitutions (Levitin, A., 2011, p.251). Gaussian elimination requires about $[n^3/3]$ multiplications. Horner's rule is an optimal algorithm for polynomial evaluation without coefficient preprocessing which requires only n multiplications and n additions to evaluate an n-degree polynomial at a given point. Horner's rule also has a few useful byproducts, such as the synthetic division algorithm.

Linear programming concerns optimizing a linear function of several variables subject to constraints in the form of linear equations and linear inequalities. There are efficient algorithms capable of solving very large instances of this problem with many thousands of variables and constraints, provided the variables are not required to be integers. The latter, called integer linear

programming, constitute a much more difficult class of problems.

2. CRITICAL CONTEXT

In general, a linear program is a problem of maximizing or minimizing a linear function of some variables subject to linear constraints on those variables. Linear programming is one of the most general problems known to be solvable in polynomial time. Many optimization problems can be cast directly as polynomial-size linear programs and thus solved in polynomial time (Khuller, S., 2012, p.83). The most common method of solving linear programs is the simplex algorithm, due to Dantzig. The method first converts the linear inequalities into equality constraints by introducing slack variables. The Primal-Dual Method is a useful tool for solving combinatorial optimization problems (Khuller, S., p.138).

Dynamic programming problems are typically optimization problems (find the minimum or maximum cost solution, subject to various constraints) (Mount, D.M., 2003, p.11). The technique is related to divide-and-conquer, in the sense that it breaks problems down into smaller problems that it solves recursively. However, because of the somewhat different nature of dynamic programming problems, standard divide-and-conquer solutions are not usually efficient. Dynamic programming typically applies to optimization problems if (1) the original problem can be divided into smaller sub-problems, and (2) the recursion among sub-problems has optimal-substructure property, i.e., the optimal solution to the original problem can be calculated through combining the optimal solutions to sub-problems. Unlike the general divide-and-conquer framework, a dynamic programming algorithm usually enumerates all possible dividing strategies. The basic elements that characterize a dynamic programming algorithm, according to Mount, D.M. (2003, p.11) are:
❖ Sub-structure, which involves decomposing the problem into smaller (and hopefully simpler) sub-problems and then expressing the solution of the original problem in terms of solutions for smaller problems.
❖ Table-structure, where the answers to the sub-problems are stored in a table since the sub-problem solutions are reused many times.

❖ Bottom-up computation, which combines the solutions on smaller sub-problems to solve larger sub-problems.

Erickson, J. (2019, p.190) formally defines a (simple) graph as a pair of sets (V, E), where V is an arbitrary non-empty finite set, whose elements are called vertices or nodes, and E is a set of pairs of elements of V, which we call edges. A graph is a collection of vertices or nodes, connected by a collection of edges (Mount, D.M., 2003, p.30). Graphs are a very flexible mathematical model for many application problems. A directed graph (or digraph) G = (V,E) consists of a finite set V, called the vertices or nodes, and E, a set of ordered pairs, called the edges of G. Put simply, E is a binary relation on V (Mount, D.M., 2003, p.30). An undirected graph (or graph) G = (V,E) consists of a finite set V of vertices, and a set E of unordered pairs of distinct vertices, called the edges. Figure 1 below shows the Digraph and Graph, respectively.

Figure 1: Digraph and Graph

Digraph   Graph

Splay trees are a powerful data structure that function as search trees without any explicit balancing conditions, and serve as an excellent tool to demonstrate the power of amortized analysis (Khuller, S., 2012, p.7). The amortized time of a splay operation is $O(\log n)$ (Khuller, S., 2012, p.10).

A planar embedding of a graph, is a mapping of the vertices and edges to the plane such that no two edges cross. A graph is said to be planar, if it has a planar embedding (Khuller, S., 2012, p.58). One can also view planar graphs as those graphs that have a planar embedding on a sphere. Planar graphs are useful since they arise in the context of VLSI design. The smallest non-planar graphs are K_5 and $K_{3,3}$ (Khuller, S., 2012, p.62).

A polynomial time algorithm is any algorithm that runs in time $O(n^k)$ where k is some constant that is independent of n. A problem is said to be solvable in polynomial time if there is a polynomial time algorithm that solves it (Mount, D.M., 2003, p.57). Let P be the class of problems that can be solved in polynomial time. We say problem X ☐ Y (X reduces to Y) if we can show the following: if there is a polynomial time algorithm for problem Y and we can use it to design a polynomial time algorithm for problem X, then X can be reduced to solving Y (Khuller, S., 2012, p.75).

NP stands for non-deterministic polynomial-time (Weiss, M.A., 2014, p.434). A deterministic machine, at each point in time, is executing an instruction. Depending on the instruction, it then goes to some next instruction, which is unique. According to Weiss, M.A. (2014, p.434), a non-deterministic machine has a choice of next step where it is free to choose any that it wishes, and if one of these steps leads to a solution, it will always choose the correct one. Among all the problems known to be in NP, there is a subset, known as the NP-complete problems, which contains the hardest. An NP-complete problem has the property that any problem in NP can be polynomially reduced to it (Weiss, M.A., 2014, p.434.

NP-completeness: A problem Q is said to be NP-complete, if we can prove (a) Q $\square$ N P and (b)
$$\forall X \in N P X \propto Q. \quad \text{(Khuller, S., 2012, p.75).}$$

In this context we define the following classes of problems:

❖ **P**: This is the set of all decision problems that can be solved in polynomial time, and these problems are generally referred to as being "easy" or "efficiently solvable" (Mount, D.M., 203, p.58).

❖ **NP:** This is the set of all decision problems that can be verified in polynomial time and contains P as a subset (Mount, D.M., 2003, p.59). The NP class contains a number of easy problems, but it also contains a number of problems that are believed to be very hard to solve. The term NP does not mean "not polynomial" but "nondeterministic polynomial time".

❖ **NP-hard:** This is a problem if we could solve this problem in polynomial time, then we could solve all NP problems in polynomial time (Mount, D.M., 2003, p.59). It must be noted here that for a problem to be NP hard, it does not have to be in the class NP. However, since it is widely believed that all NP problems are not solvable in polynomial time, it is widely believed that no NP-hard problem is solvable in polynomial time.

❖ **NP-complete:** A problem is NP-complete if (1) it is in NP, and (2) it is NP-hard.
That is, NPC = NP∩NP-hard.

Reduction is the single most common technique used in designing algorithms. Reducing one problem X to another problem Y means to write an algorithm for X that uses an algorithm for Y as a black box or subroutine (Erickson, J., 2019, p.921). Crucially, the correctness of the resulting algorithm for X cannot depend in any way on how the algorithm for Y works. Erickson, J. (2019, p.22) stated that when we design algorithms, we may not know exactly how the basic building blocks we use are implemented, or how our algorithms might be used as building blocks to solve even bigger problems. *Recursion* is a particularly powerful kind of reduction, which according to Erickson, J. (2019, p.22), can be described loosely as follows :
• If the given instance of the problem can be solved directly, solve it directly.
• Otherwise, reduce it to one or more simpler instances of the same problem.

3. INTEGRATIVE CONCLUSION

The paper presented an analytical exposition, critical context and integrative conclusion on the the six major text books on Algorithms Design and Analysis. An algorithm is a sequence of unambiguous instructions for solving a problem, i.e., for obtaining a required output for any legitimate input in a finite amount of time (Levitin, A., 2011, p.3). Algorithms can be considered as procedural solutions to problems where the focus is on correctness and efficiency (Mount, D.M., 2003, p.2). The important problem types are sorting, searching, string processing, graph problems, combinatorial problems, geometric problems, and numerical problems. Both time and space efficiencies are measured as functions of the algorithm's input size. The efficiencies of a large number of algorithms fall into the following few classes: constant, logarithmic, linear, linearithmic, quadratic, cubic, and exponential (Levitin, A., 2011, p.95). *Time complexity* is a measure of time efficiency which indicates how fast an algorithm in question runs. *Space complexity* measures the space efficiency, which is the amount of memory units required by the algorithm in addition to the space needed for its input and output (Levitin, A., 2011, p.42). The worst-case efficiency of an algorithm is its efficiency which the algorithm runs the longest among all possible inputs of that size n (Levitin, A., 2011, p.47). The best-case efficiency of an algorithm is its efficiency which the algorithm runs the fastest among all possible inputs of that size (Levitin, A., 2011, p.48).

Divide-and-conquer is a general algorithm design technique that solves a problem by dividing it into several smaller sub-problems of the same type and about the same size, solving each of them recursively, and then combining their solutions to get a solution to the original problem (Levitin, A., 2011, p.198). Many efficient algorithms are based on this technique, although it can be both inapplicable and inferior to simpler algorithmic solutions. Mergesort is a divide-and-conquer sorting algorithm, which works by dividing an input array into two halves, sorting them recursively, and then merging the two sorted halves to get the original array sorted (Levitin, A., 2011, p.198). Quicksort is a divide-and-conquer sorting algorithm that works by partitioning its input elements according to their value relative to some preselected element (Levitin, 2011, p.168). Quicksort is noted for its superior efficiency among n log n algorithms for sorting randomly ordered arrays but also for the quadratic worst-case efficiency. A sorting algorithm is stable if two elements that are equal remain in the same relative position after sorting is completed (Mount, D.M., 2003, p.8). Decrease-and-conquer is a general algorithm design technique, based on exploiting a relationship between a solution to a given instance of a problem and a solution to a smaller instance of the same problem.

A problem is said to be solvable in polynomial time if there is a polynomial time algorithm that solves it (Mount, D.M., 2003, p.57). Let P be the class of problems that can be solved in polynomial time. NP stands for non-deterministic polynomial-time (Weiss, M.A., 2014, p.434). A deterministic machine, at each point in time, is executing an instruction.

Bibliography

ERICKSON, J. (2019). Algorithms, Creative Commons, ISBN: 978-1-792-64483-2 (paperback), © Copyright 2019 Jeff Erickson, Creative Commons Attribution 4.0 International License, http://jeffe.cs.illinois.edu/teaching/algorithms/

KLEINBERG, J., and Tardos, E., (2005). Algorithm Design, Pearson Education, Inc., 2006, ISBN 0-321-29535-8 (alk. paper).

KHULLER, S., (2012). Design and Analysis of Algorithms: Course Notes, Dept. of Computer Science, University of Maryland, January 26, 2012

LEVITIN, A., (2011). Introduction to the design & analysis of algorithms: 3rd Edition, Pearson, New York, 2015, ISBN-13: 978-0-13-231681-1, ISBN-10: 0-13-231681-1.

MOUNT, D.M., (2003). Design and Analysis of Computer Algorithms, Department of Computer Science, University of Maryland, Fall 2003.

WEISS, M.A., (2014). Data structures and algorithm analysis in C++, Fourth Edition, Florida International University, ISBN-13: 978-0-13-284737-7 (alk. paper), ISBN-10: 0-13-284737-X (alk. paper), QA76.73.C153W46 2014.

YOUR KNOWLEDGE HAS VALUE

- We will publish your bachelor's and master's thesis, essays and papers

- Your own eBook and book - sold worldwide in all relevant shops

- Earn money with each sale

Upload your text at www.GRIN.com
and publish for free

www.ingramcontent.com/pod-product-compliance
Lightning Source LLC
La Vergne TN
LVHW042322060326
832902LV00010B/1684